Original title:
Loving from the Inside Out

Copyright © 2024 Swan Charm
All rights reserved.

Author: Linda Leevike
ISBN HARDBACK: 978-9916-89-268-8
ISBN PAPERBACK: 978-9916-89-269-5
ISBN EBOOK: 978-9916-89-270-1

Pillars of Inner Strength

In the silence of the storm,
We find our roots, we feel the form.
With courage built on hope's own stone,
We rise as one, never alone.

Each challenge faced, each tear embraced,
For wisdom grows, not gone to waste.
From shadows past, our light will beam,
In unity, we chase the dream.

Blossoming from Within

In the garden of the soul,
A seed is sown, a hidden goal.
With patience, we begin to see,
A lovely bloom, our own decree.

The petals spread, in colors bright,
Each scent released, pure delight.
Through trials faced, and fears outgrown,
The beauty thrives, our seeds are sown.

The Glow of Self-Embrace

In the mirror's gentle gaze,
We find the truth of tender ways.
With every flaw and every scar,
We shine the brightest, just as we are.

Embracing all, the love we show,
Creates a warmth that starts to glow.
Within ourselves, we learn to trust,
In self-compassion, find the must.

Life's Inner Melody

In whispers soft, the heart does sing,
With every note, a delicate ring.
The rhythm flows through breath and beat,
In harmony, we find our seat.

Amidst the noise, we find our tune,
A dance with stars, beneath the moon.
Through ups and downs, our song prevails,
In life's sweet symphony, love entails.

The Revelation of My Heart

In whispers soft, my heart will speak,
Unraveling truths that make me weak.
Each beat a note in life's grand score,
Revealing love, I can't ignore.

With every glance, the world ignites,
A spark of hope in endless nights.
Through trials faced and dreams set free,
My heart unfolds its melody.

Inner Journeys of Warmth

In quiet realms where shadows play,
I find the light to guide my way.
Each step I take, a dance with grace,
Inner warmth, my sacred space.

Through fears untamed, I start to rise,
Within me bloom the stars and skies.
With every breath, I feel reborn,
A gentle heart where love is sworn.

The Symphony of Loving Self

In harmony, my soul takes flight,
A symphony of pure delight.
Each note a thread woven with care,
A celebration of love laid bare.

Embracing flaws, I find my song,
A melody that's bold and strong.
In every chord, I learn to be,
A loving self, wild and free.

Dancing with the Spirit Within

In rhythms soft, the spirit sways,
Guiding me through the golden rays.
With open arms, I join the dance,
Embracing life, a sacred chance.

Through every twirl, I lose the ground,
In joyful leaps, my soul is found.
With every breath, I feel the call,
To dance with spirit, give my all.

The Light of Inner Affection

In twilight's glow, hearts softly beam,
Kindred spirits weave a gentle dream.
Through whispered words, love's whispers flow,
A radiant bond, in silence we grow.

In tender moments, shadows fall away,
With every glance, hopes begin to sway.
The warmth of touch, a soothing embrace,
Ignites the spark, that time can't erase.

As laughter dances beneath the sky,
We build our world where souls can fly.
In harmony, we share our truth,
The light of affection proves our youth.

Through trials faced, our spirits combine,
In our hearts, a love that's divine.
The bonds we cherish, forever will bind,
The light of affection, uniquely designed.

In every heartbeat, a story unfolds,
With patience and care, our universe molds.
The light within, an everlasting glow,
A treasure of love, we joyfully sow.

Threads of Self-Revelation

In quiet moments, truth starts to rise,
Unraveling layers, beneath tangled skies.
Each thread we pull, a memory appears,
Crafting our story through laughter and tears.

In the tapestry, colors intertwine,
The essence of self, a design so fine.
Through trials faced, we begin to see,
The beauty of being who we dare to be.

With every heartbeat, whispers ignite,
Calling us forth, into the light.
Threads of self, a delicate dance,
Inviting the world to join in the chance.

As shadows fade and clarity grows,
We embrace our truth, like a river that flows.
The journey within, a sacred unfold,
With threads of self, our stories are told.

In every stitch, a lesson we've found,
In the fabric of life, our spirits are bound.
Through threads of revelation, we come to be,
The masterpiece woven in unity.

Symphony of the Inner Voice

In whispers soft, a call to rise,
Echoes dance beneath the skies.
A melody that stirs the heart,
Guiding me to play my part.

Notes of courage, fears laid bare,
Resonating through the air.
With every beat, the truth unfolds,
A symphony of dreams retold.

Tides of Self-Realization

Waves of thought, they ebb and flow,
Washing secrets we don't show.
A shoreline where reflections lie,
Beneath the vast and open sky.

Each crest brings light, each trough brings peace,
In the depths, my doubts release.
As currents shift, I come to see,
The endless depths that flow in me.

The Canvas of My Spirit

Colors blend in vibrant hue,
Strokes of life, both bold and true.
With every brush, I claim the space,
Creating worlds, I find my grace.

Canvas stretched, yet free to roam,
In this art, I find my home.
A portrait of the soul's embrace,
Imprinted with love, time, and grace.

Embracing the Unheard Songs

In silence deep, a song awakes,
Notes of joy that fear forsakes.
With gentle hands, I hold the sound,
In every breath, the truth is found.

Melodies of battles won,
Whispers of the rising sun.
Through shadows cast, I see the light,
Embracing songs that spark the night.

From Core to Cosmos

In the depths where silence sleeps,
Whispers of the universe creep.
From the heart's quiet glow,
Stars begin to ebb and flow.

Through roots that grasp the ground,
We seek what can be found.
Connecting all that is,
A dance of cosmic bliss.

From the core to skies above,
Every pulse, a sign of love.
Galaxies spin and swirl,
In the heart, the universe unfurls.

The Inner Light's Journey

Within the shadows, a spark ignites,
Guiding souls through long, dark nights.
The inner light, a gentle flame,
Leading us through joy and pain.

Step by step, the path unfolds,
Stories of the brave and bold.
Through valleys deep, we wander wide,
With our light as faithful guide.

In every heart, a beacon glows,
Shattering doubt and all our woes.
Together we rise, hand in hand,
In this shared, luminous land.

Blossoms of Self-Acceptance

Petals soft, in sunlight's grace,
Fragrance whispers, we embrace.
In gardens wild, we choose to grow,
Learning to love the seeds we sow.

Each flaw a mark of history,
Painting our shared tapestry.
Regrets, like shadows, softly fade,
In the warmth that we have made.

Embracing all that we have been,
Transforming pain to gentle kin.
In every bloom, a story told,
Of courage found, and hearts made bold.

Embracing the Unseen

In the quiet, secrets lie,
Invisible threads that weave the sky.
A touch, a glance, a fleeting thought,
The unseen battles bravely fought.

We gather strength from silent dreams,
Where hope flows like gentle streams.
In shadows dark, reside the wise,
Whispers of truths, we recognize.

Embrace the depths that cannot show,
For there, the seeds of love will grow.
In the void, we find our grace,
A dance of souls in timeless space.

Abiding Spirit

In the quiet of night, we find our peace,
Hope whispers softly, worries cease.
Guiding light within us all,
Rising strong, we will not fall.

Through the storms, the shadows loom,
Yet love's warmth will always bloom.
Hearts entwined, we walk this road,
Together we'll share the load.

With every breath, we seek the truth,
In laughter shared, we find our youth.
Abiding spirit, ever near,
In our journey, cast aside fear.

As stars emerge in evening's glow,
We hold our dreams, let them flow.
Endless horizons call our name,
Together we rise, never the same.

So take my hand, let's fly away,
To distant lands where hearts can sway.
With every step, we grow more wise,
In the promise of tomorrow's skies.

Colors of the Heart Within

In shades of red, the passion burns,
A dance of flames, a heart that yearns.
Golden hues of joy arise,
In laughter shared, beneath bright skies.

The cool blue whispers secrets shared,
In moments still, our souls laid bare.
Green of hope in every dream,
A canvas bright, we paint our theme.

Violet whispers of love's embrace,
Soft and tender, a gentle pace.
Each color tells a tale so vast,
From shadows deep, to joy that lasts.

We weave the colors, day by day,
In vivid strokes, we find our way.
Emotions burst like flowers in spring,
Each tint a note in life's sweet sing.

Together we create our art,
With every brush, we play our part.
Forever in this vibrant dance,
Colors of the heart, our timeless chance.

Nestled Emotions

In the quiet corners of our hearts,
Nestled softly, love imparts.
Whispers linger, tales unfold,
In warmth we find our stories told.

Gentle waves of joy arise,
As laughter twinkles in the skies.
In shadows, tears may softly flow,
Yet resilience will always grow.

Hopes are cradled, dreams take flight,
In the depths of the enchanting night.
Every heartbeat, every sigh,
Speaks of love that never dies.

Tender moments, fleeting grace,
In each embrace, we find our place.
So close your eyes and breathe it in,
Nestled emotions, where love begins.

With every dawn, new joys appear,
As the sun breaks through the tear.
Together forever, we shall stand,
In this life, hand in hand.

The Soul's Embrace

In the depths of silence, hearts align,
A sacred bond, a love divine.
With every glance, the spirit soars,
Together we unlock love's doors.

Through every trial, we learn and grow,
In gentle whispers, our truth flows.
With open arms, we welcome fate,
In the dance of love, we resonate.

The warmth of souls, a cosmic thread,
In every joy, in every dread.
We share the light, we share the pain,
In the soul's embrace, there's much to gain.

Time may shift like grains of sand,
Yet love is steady, hand in hand.
As seasons change, our hearts remain,
In this embrace, forever sustained.

So close your eyes and feel the glow,
A deeper love, we'll always know.
In every moment, grace will find,
The soul's embrace, eternally kind.

Embrace of the Inner Flame

In the silence, sparks ignite,
Warmth and glow, a guiding light.
Through the shadows, courage grows,
In the heart, the spirit knows.

Fuel the fire, let it burn bright,
Feel the rush, embrace the night.
With each flicker, dreams take flight,
In this dance, we find our sight.

Whispers echo, soft and clear,
In the stillness, cast your fear.
From the depths, the truth will climb,
In the embrace of the inner rhyme.

Hold the flame, let it inspire,
In the chaos, find your fire.
With each challenge, each refrain,
We shine brighter, unchained and sane.

Together we rise, hearts in tune,
Under the watch of the silver moon.
In the forest of our shared desire,
We are embers, we are fire.

Heartstrings Unveiled

In the twilight, hearts collide,
Threads of fate, we cannot hide.
With every glance, a story sewn,
In the silence, love is known.

Gentle whispers, soft confessions,
Tangled roots, hidden expressions.
Through the storms, our truth will sail,
In the dance of heartstrings unveiled.

With each heartbeat, memories rise,
Capturing dreams, under starlit skies.
In the embrace of timeless grace,
Love transcends, we find our place.

Seasons change, yet we remain,
In the laughter, in the pain.
Through the echoes of joy and wail,
Forever bound, heartstrings unveil.

In the tapestry of night's embrace,
We weave our love, in sacred space.
With every note, let the harmony flow,
Together as one, let our spirits glow.

Whispers of the Soul

In the dawn, secrets unfold,
Whispers soft, stories told.
Through the mist, a voice transcends,
In our hearts, the journey bends.

Lost in thoughts, gently stride,
In the silence, dreams confide.
With each heartbeat, truth takes form,
In the whispers, we transform.

Echoing through the quiet night,
Guiding stars, our inner light.
With each breath, we rise and fall,
In the shadows, we stand tall.

Every sigh, a tale to share,
In this bond, we lay ourselves bare.
With the moon as our guiding compass,
Our spirits dance in shared promise.

Let the whispers lead the way,
Through the night, into the day.
With each step, our souls entwine,
In the journey, we align.

Radiance Beneath the Surface

Beneath the waves, a light so bright,
Hidden depths, out of sight.
In the currents, dreams reside,
Radiance blooms, like the tide.

Ripples dance, in a secret flow,
Guiding paths where few will go.
With each heartbeat, layers peel,
In the depths, we start to heal.

Underneath, a world alive,
In shadows deep, our hopes survive.
Through the darkness, visions rise,
Radiance gleams, beyond the lies.

Let the waves carry your fears,
In the quiet, silence hears.
With each breath, embrace the change,
To find the light, often strange.

In the journey, we unearth,
The treasures found in our rebirth.
With radiance bright, let's traverse,
The hidden depth, our universe.

Tapestry of the Heart

In the loom of night, dreams weave,
Colors bright, in silence, believe.
Threads of joy, and whispers of pain,
A tapestry formed, love's sweet refrain.

Moments stitched, with every glance,
Fate entwined in a fragile dance.
Patterns shift, yet the heart remains,
Bound by whispers, etched in veins.

In every thread, a story lies,
Softened cries and laughter's skies.
With every tug, the fabric bends,
A timeless tale, where love transcends.

Silken strands of hope unite,
Holding close through endless flight.
In the weave, secrets softly part,
The intricate work of the heart.

Crafted gently, with hands so wise,
Beneath the stars, where the spirit flies.
Each fiber tells of joy and strife,
The beauty of this woven life.

Unseen Threads of Warmth

Beneath the surface, calm and still,
Hidden warmth, a potent thrill.
Threads unseen bind us tight,
Growing stronger in the night.

With every smile, connection grows,
In gentle gestures, love bestows.
A shared glance, an open heart,
Unseen threads always play their part.

In quiet moments, bonds are spun,
Brighter than the midday sun.
Through trials faced, through laughter shared,\nThese
threads of warmth show we have cared.

Like morning dew on blades of grass,
A silent strength will always last.
Together woven, we find our place,
In unseen warmth, we embrace grace.

Each connection, a sacred thread,
In the fabric of life, lightly tread.
Through unseen ties, we shall remain,
Embraced by warmth, beyond the pain.

Soulful Serenade

In the moonlit night, songs arise,
Melodies dance, beneath the skies.
Notes of sorrow, joy intertwine,
A soulful serenade, truly divine.

With every chord, emotions flow,
In harmony, hearts start to glow.
The music carries us above,
A gentle whisper, a tale of love.

Voices blend, like rivers' grace,
Winding softly, through time and space.
Each note a brush on canvas wide,
A soulful serenade, where hearts confide.

Beneath the stars, the echoes ring,
In silent pauses, our spirits sing.
With every rhythm, we find our way,
To the melody of a brand new day.

Together weaving the sound of dreams,
In every pause, the heart redeems.
The soulful serenade shall be our guide,
Through life's grand stage, where we abide.

Finding Light in Shadows

In the depths, where shadows dwell,
Cloaked in silence, a whispered spell.
Yet from the dark, a spark ignites,
A beacon found, in the quiet nights.

With every stumble, strength is gained,
Through the shadows, hope is maintained.
The heart's resolve, a steady flame,
Guiding us through, as we reclaim.

In tangled paths, the fears dissolve,
As we seek light, our souls evolve.
The weight of night, a fleeting test,
In shadows deep, we find our quest.

For every heart that learns to fight,
In troubled times, we find our light.
Through shifting forms, the dawn will break,
Finding solace, for hope's sweet sake.

As shadows fade, and daylight streams,
We rise anew, fulfilled with dreams.
With open hearts, we journey on,
Finding light, till the shadows are gone.

Silhouettes of Inner Bliss

In the quiet shades of dawn,
Soft whispers fade away the night.
Dreams take flight on gentle wings,
A dance of shadows in soft light.

Moments linger, time stands still,
In the embrace of morning's haze.
Colors blend and hearts collide,
In the hush of this tranquil phase.

Reflections glimmer like the stars,
Hidden truths begin to shine.
Every heartbeat sings a song,
Of love that's pure and divine.

With each pulse, the spirit wakes,
Boundless joy flows through the veins.
In the echoes of laughter shared,
All sorrow gently wanes.

Silhouettes of dreams alive,
Reveal the essence of the soul.
In stillness where the heart takes root,
We find our way, we become whole.

Notes of a Heartfelt Journey

As I tread this winding road,
With weary feet and heavy sighs,
I gather notes of every joy,
And treasure tears that softly rise.

Each step a story yet untold,
The laughter dances in the breeze.
With every turn, a lesson learned,
Nature whispers, 'Take it ease.'

Through echoes of a distant love,
I embrace the warmth of fleeting days.
Moments freeze, forever held,
In the folds of time's gentle ways.

The symphony of life unfolds,
With highs and lows, a grand design.
I hold the notes within my heart,
In every struggle, love will shine.

And as the sun begins to set,
I'll spread my wings, embrace the sky.
For every step brings me closer still,
To the dreams I'll never deny.

Whispered Promises to Self

In the mirror, I face my truth,
Soft whispers fill the silent space.
Promises kissed with gentle hope,
That guide me to a warmer place.

When shadows stretch and doubts arise,
I anchor deep within my light.
Every word a soothing balm,
In moments dark, I find my might.

I vow to cherish all my scars,
For they map out the path I've tread.
With each breath, I choose to rise,
Embracing all the dreams I've fed.

The heart speaks loudly, learns to trust,
In solitude, I find my song.
Whispers weave a tapestry,
Of strength that's carried all along.

With every dawn, new vows I make,
To love myself with tender grace.
In the quiet, I find my peace,
And know that I belong, my space.

The Stillness of Self-Affection

Within the silence, love awakes,
A gentle touch of soft embrace.
I find the beauty hidden deep,
In the quiet of this sacred space.

A tender heart beats loud and clear,
Each pulse a song, sweet and true.
In the stillness, strength is found,
As whispers of love begin to brew.

I cultivate the seeds of peace,
In every thought, a bloom so bright.
With gratitude, I weave my days,
In the tapestry of purest light.

Moments linger, time holds fast,
And in this realm, I learn to trust.
For self-affection guides my way,
In this journey, I am robust.

As echoes fade and shadows slip,
I celebrate the love I gain.
In the stillness, there I'll stay,
Embracing joy amidst the rain.

Inner Glow

In the silence of the night,
A spark begins to shine,
Warmth wraps around the heart,
Embracing every line.

Whispers echo softly here,
Dreams that rise and flow,
Each moment, pure and near,
Nurtured by inner glow.

Flickering flames of hope,
Illuminate the dark,
As we learn to cope,
With love's enduring spark.

Through shadows we will wander,
Finding peace in grace,
Every thought brings wonder,
In this sacred space.

Together we will stand,
Hand in hand, so brave,
Creating with our minds,
A world we long to save.

Outer Grace

Gentle breezes kiss the trees,
Underneath the sky,
A dance of leaves plays with ease,
Nature's sweet lullaby.

With each step we tread anew,
Footprints soft and light,
In the morning's vivid hue,
We embrace the pure sight.

Flowers bloom in every shade,
Colors bright and rare,
In this beauty, love is made,
Magic lingers in the air.

Stars will guide us through the night,
Winking in their place,
The universe holds us tight,
Wrapped in outer grace.

With each moment, peace surrounds,
Harmony is near,
In the silence, love abounds,
Washing away all fear.

Threads of Connection

Woven through the fabric tight,
Lives intersect and blend,
In the tapestry of light,
We find and help amend.

Voices rise in joyful song,
Each note a gentle thread,
Together we will grow strong,
With every word we spread.

In simple acts, we find our place,
A helping hand we lend,
Unity in every face,
With love, our true transcend.

From the heart, we reach beyond,
Creating bonds so pure,
In this dance, we all respond,
To be kind and endure.

Together we can weave a dream,
Of hope and gentle spark,
In this vast and wondrous scheme,
We illuminate the dark.

The Pulse of Kindness

In the heart, a rhythm beats,
A pulse that knows no bounds,
With every smile, love repeats,
In every heart, it sounds.

Gentle touch, a gesture warm,
Ripples spread wide and far,
In the storm, we find our calm,
Like a guiding star.

Words of love can mend the pain,
As rain brings life anew,
In simple acts, we break the chain,
Of sorrow, brave and true.

Together, we can share the load,
Each step a tiny flame,
In kindness, we find the road,
To heal, to break the shame.

May our hearts with kindness swell,
In every darkened space,
With love's rhythm, we will dwell,
In the pulse of our grace.

Fortress of Tenderness

Behind the walls, a haven lies,
Built of trust and care,
In quiet moments, love will rise,
A fortress strong and rare.

Soft whispers in the night,
Embracing every soul,
In this space, we find our light,
As kindness takes its toll.

With every hug, a shield we form,
Shielding hearts from pain,
In the storm, we are the warm,
Safe from life's disdain.

Through trials, we will journey on,
With laughter leading us,
In every setting sun and dawn,
In love, we trust and fuss.

Together in this cherished place,
United, we are strong,
Within this fortress, we embrace,
And in our hearts, belong.

Heartbeats in Harmony

In quiet moments, we align,
Each heartbeat echoing a sign.
Together in a world so wide,
With every thump, we feel the tide.

As rhythms dance in soft embrace,
Life unfolds at a steady pace.
With friends beside and love in tow,
We find the strength to let love grow.

Through every trial, through every test,
In harmony, we find our rest.
In whispered dreams and gentle sighs,
Our hearts unite beneath the skies.

For every laughter, every tear,
In heartbeats shared, we conquer fear.
An unseen bond that we create,
In rhythm's pulse, we celebrate.

Together forged, our souls entwined,
In harmony, our hearts aligned.
With every moment passing by,
We write our story, you and I.

The Alchemy of Inner Peace

In stillness blessed, the mind releases,
The worries fall like autumn leaves.
With breath as guide, we find our way,
In inner calm, we choose to stay.

Moments woven, soft and light,
Transforming darkness into bright.
With each exhale, let go the fear,
In peace we learn to hold what's dear.

Through whispered thoughts, and gentle care,
A sanctuary built in air.
Where chaos fades and joy ignites,
We find our hearts in quiet nights.

The world may rush, but we will pause,
In sacred space, we find our cause.
With gratitude, we open wide,
The alchemy where peace resides.

For every heartbeat, every breath,
In stillness, we embrace our depth.
With open hearts, we seek release,
In every moment, find our peace.

Tapestry of Self-Discovery

Threads of colors, stories spun,
In each encounter, battles won.
A tapestry of dreams unfolds,
In every tale, the heart beholds.

With every step, a lesson learned,
In twists and turns, the soul returned.
Through mirrors held, reflection's grace,
In every fiber, we find our place.

With courage bold, we weave our truth,
In vibrant shades, we honor youth.
The patterns shift, the colors blend,
In self-discovery, we ascend.

Each patch a memory dear to hold,
As we embrace the brave and bold.
In layers deep, we come to see,
The beauty found in being free.

So let us stitch with threads of light,
In every shadow, find the bright.
In this grand weave, we find our part,
A tapestry, a work of heart.

The Glow from Within

A flicker sparks, a candle's light,
From deep inside, it burns so bright.
With every thought that dares to rise,
We shine like stars in dusky skies.

In quiet moments, warmth bestowed,
The inner glow begins to unfold.
As courage blooms in shades of gold,
Our stories shine, a truth retold.

With every heartbeat, every spark,
We light the shadows, banish dark.
In unity, we find our strength,
Our glow expands in perfect length.

Each kindness shared, a luminous thread,
In every smile, our spirits fed.
Together casting warmth around,
In every heart, a home is found.

So let it shine, this inner flame,
A guiding light, it knows our name.
With love ignited, we will begin,
To live and love from deep within.

Hearth of Connections

In the glow of warming fire,
Laughter dances with desire.
Voices rise like gentle smoke,
Each word a bond, our hearts invoke.

Together we share dreams and fears,
Building bridges with our tears.
Hands held tight in trust and grace,
In this haven, our hearts embrace.

Memories linger, sweet and bright,
In the soft and calming light.
Each moment a precious thread,
Woven tight, where love is spread.

Through trials and paths we roam,
This hearth forever feels like home.
In every encounter, we find our way,
Binding us closer, come what may.

So let the flames burn steady and true,
In this sacred space, just me and you.
With every story, our spirits soar,
In the hearth of connections, we ask for more.

Where Hearts Intertwine

Underneath the starlit sky,
Two souls meet, and spirits fly.
Every glance, a silent vow,
In this moment, here and now.

We wander through the whispered night,
Hand in hand, hearts full of light.
With every laugh, a spark ignites,
In this dance, our love takes flight.

Paths may twist and turn away,
But together, we'll choose to stay.
In the shadows, we find our grace,
Where hearts intertwine, we find our place.

Through the storms and through the calm,
In your embrace, I feel the balm.
With each heartbeat, we define,
This sacred space, where hearts intertwine.

As dawn approaches, skies expand,
Forever bound, we make our stand.
In the silence, hear the sign,
For in this love, our hearts entwine.

Inward Radiance

In the mirror of my soul,
I find the pieces that make me whole.
Shadows fade with every glance,
Inward radiant, in love's dance.

Every heartbeat, a gentle glow,
Illuminates the path I know.
Embracing all that lies within,
In this journey, I begin.

The whispers of my heart take flight,
Guiding me through darkest night.
In stillness, I hear the call,
Inward radiance shines through all.

Through the layers, truth unfolds,
Within my core, a story told.
Each moment, a spark divine,
Illuminating love's design.

The beauty lies in purest light,
Inward radiance feels so right.
With every step, I walk the line,
Embracing joy, let love's light shine.

The Core of Affection

In the stillness, love awakes,
Quiet moments, soft heart breaks.
Each heartbeat, a gentle reminder,
The core of affection, sweet and kinder.

Among the chaos, find the calm,
In your arms, I find my balm.
Through every challenge, we remain,
Bound together, through joy and pain.

Whispers linger, soft and dear,
In our laughter, we hold near.
In shadows cast by fleeting time,
The core of affection, pure and prime.

Through seasons that ebb and flow,
In the depths, our love will grow.
With every sunrise, hearts align,
In this union, the world is fine.

So let the echoes of our song,
Remind us where our hearts belong.
Forever in this sacred space,
The core of affection, our embrace.

The Essence of Us

In quiet whispers, we collide,
Two souls entwined, a surging tide.
With every glance, a spark ignites,
Our hearts in tune, like stars at nights.

Together we dance, a timeless waltz,
Unraveling fate, erasing faults.
Your laughter echoes, a sweet refrain,
In every joy, I find my gain.

The world may change, but we will stay,
In this embrace, come what may.
Through storms and sun, we find our way,
A love that thrives, day after day.

With every heartbeat, a promise made,
In shadows cast, our fears will fade.
The essence of us, a vibrant hue,
Boundless love, forever true.

So let us journey, hand in hand,
In fields of dreams, on golden sand.
Forever we'll be, in harmony spun,
Two souls as one, forever begun.

Inner Symphony of Devotion

In the hush of night, pure chords arise,
Melodies weave 'neath starlit skies.
Each note a pledge, a sacred vow,
In silence shared, we learn just how.

With gentle hands, we paint the air,
Filling the space with love and care.
Every heartbeat plays a tune,
A symphony blessed beneath the moon.

Through trials faced, our voices blend,
An endless song that will not end.
In every glance, the music swells,
As stories of our souls it tells.

Wrapped in echoes, we find our peace,
A harmony that will never cease.
The inner symphony flows free,
In every moment, just you and me.

Let others hear our sacred song,
As in each verse, we both belong.
In devotion's arms, we find our grace,
A melody time cannot erase.

Nexus of Nurtured Feelings

In gardens where emotions bloom,
We plant our hopes, dispelling gloom.
Each seed a whisper, softly sown,
In the nexus where love has grown.

Through seasons' change, we tend with care,
Watering dreams we both can share.
With patience warm, the bond we feed,
In every moment, love takes heed.

A tapestry woven of trust so fine,
In every thread, your heart entwines.
In laughter's light, and sorrow's shade,
The nexus holds the vows we've made.

As time unfolds, and shadows shift,
Our nurtured feelings are the gift.
A connection deep, like roots below,
In every heartbeat, love will grow.

So here we stand, hand in hand,
In this sacred union, we will stand.
Together we thrive, strong and true,
Every moment, just me and you.

Within the Heart's Embrace

In the quiet dawn, our spirits rise,
With gentle warmth, beneath the skies.
Within the heart where secrets stay,
Love finds its voice and leads the way.

In every smile, a world unfurls,
With tender grace, our hearts it twirls.
Through every challenge that we meet,
Together we are, in love's heartbeat.

As shadows dance, we'll stand as one,
Beneath the stars, until we're done.
Within the heart, a sacred space,
Where every tear, finds soft embrace.

In whispers shared, and glances sought,
The binding threads of love are wrought.
Each moment cherished, a fragile thread,
In the heart's embrace, we both are led.

So let us dream, let worries cease,
In every heartbeat, we find peace.
For in the depths, where love takes place,
We'll find forever, within this space.

Heartstrings of Truth

In whispers soft, the heart does speak,
A language pure, the soul to seek.
Bound by threads that cannot break,
Each note a promise, love we make.

Through shadows deep, the light shines bright,
In darkest hours, we find our sight.
Together strong, we rise and stand,
With truth in heart, we hold each hand.

Our feelings flow like rivers wide,
In currents deep, our spirits glide.
No chains can bind, no fear can sway,
For in our truth, we find the way.

With every tear, a lesson learned,
In every joy, a fire burned.
With heartstrings twined, we face the storm,
In genuine love, our lives transform.

The Dance of Inner Radiance

In twilight's hush, our spirits sway,
A dance of light, casting shadows gray.
With every move, the cosmos sighs,
As we embrace, the universe flies.

Under the moon, we find our song,
A melody sweet, where we belong.
In vibrant hues, our hearts ignite,
As stars align, our dreams take flight.

Each twirl unfolds a story told,
In timeless rhythms, the brave and bold.
With every breath, a spark we share,
In joyful leaps, we conquer despair.

Through gentle steps, we cultivate,
A world of love that won't abate.
In this grand dance, we find our grace,
The inner light, our warm embrace.

Echoing Love's Embrace

In quiet spaces, love's echoes ring,
A tender sound, a soothing fling.
In every heartbeat, a rhythm flows,
In woven dreams, our longing grows.

Upon the winds, a whisper calls,
Through ancient woods, where silence falls.
With every glance, a story shared,
The warmth of love, forever paired.

Through mountains high, our spirits soar,
In valleys deep, we find the core.
The pulse of life, a symphony,
In tandem hearts, we find the key.

A tapestry, of moments spent,
In woven paths, our souls content.
Together bound, come what may,
In love's embrace, we find our way.

Shimmering Essence Within

In secret chambers, still and deep,
A shimmering light, in silence, weep.
Each flicker bright, a spark of grace,
In the soul's mirror, we find our place.

With every breath, the essence glows,
A hidden strength, that ever grows.
Through trials faced, we learn to shine,
In darkness found, our hearts entwine.

In layers shed, we find what's true,
A vibrant hue, of me and you.
Through gentle touch, the soul ignites,
In quiet moments, we reach new heights.

The radiance flows, an endless stream,
In unity, we dare to dream.
With every dawn, a chance to see,
The shimmering essence that sets us free.

Hand in Hand with Acceptance

In shadows where doubts often lie,
We stand together, you and I.
With gentle whispers, we let fears roam,
Hand in hand, we find our home.

Through storms that threaten to divide,
We build a bridge that will not hide.
With every struggle, we learn to grow,
Acceptance blooms, a steady glow.

With open hearts and open minds,
We weave the fabric life unwinds.
Through twists and turns, we learn to dance,
In every moment, we take a chance.

No more burdens, just love's embrace,
In every challenge, we find grace.
Together, we conquer, side by side,
Hand in hand, we shall abide.

In silence, we hear each other's song,
Through trials, our spirits grow strong.
With every heartbeat, we understand,
Together, we flourish, hand in hand.

The Heart's Hidden Light

In the stillness of a quiet night,
The heart reveals its secret light.
Amid fears and shadows, it starts to shine,
A beacon of love, endlessly divine.

Through pain and struggle, it learns to heal,
In every moment, it dares to feel.
With wings of hope, it starts to soar,
Illuminating paths, forevermore.

In whispered truths, we find our worth,
Awakening wisdom, a rebirth.
Each heartbeat echoes, a tender song,
The heart's hidden light, where we belong.

With kindness wrapped in every beat,
Love's gentle touch makes us complete.
In vulnerability, strength takes flight,
Embracing our flaws, we shine so bright.

So let us wander, hand in hand,
Under the stars, across this land.
For within each soul, a light ignites,
A symphony of hearts, bold and bright.

Fragments of Self-Love

In mirrors that hold our fractured dreams,
We gather fragments, or so it seems.
With every piece, a story unfolds,
Self-love whispers gently, brave and bold.

Through tender moments, we learn to see,
The beauty in our own company.
In scars and stories written deep,
Resilience awakens from its sleep.

Every flaw becomes a part of art,
A mosaic woven from the heart.
In acceptance, we find sweet release,
Embracing our truth brings inner peace.

With every dawn, a chance to rise,
To celebrate the light in our eyes.
In self-compassion, we find our way,
Fragments of love in the light of day.

So let the echoes of kindness play,
In the symphony of life's ballet.
For within each fragment, we discover,
The magic of being our own lover.

A Journey to the Core

In the depths where silence breathes,
A journey starts beneath the leaves.
With every step, we face the unknown,
In the heart's chamber, we find our own.

Winding paths through shadows deep,
Our secrets hidden, ours to keep.
With courage forged in the fires of pain,
We gather strength, though lost, we gain.

Each heartbeat whispers tales untold,
In the labyrinth where dreams unfold.
Through echoes of laughter, sorrow too,
We carve the way, both old and new.

As layers peel, the truth ignites,
A vivid flame, our inner sights.
In this journey, we learn to explore,
With every breath, we journey to the core.

So let us wander, with hearts so bold,
Through valleys rich and mountains gold.
For in this voyage, hand in hand,
We find our essence, our promised land.

Heart-Made Bonds

In the weave of laughter, threads combine,
Shared moments glisten, pure and fine.
Hands clasp tightly through storm and sun,
Together we rise, our hearts are one.

In whispered secrets, trust takes flight,
A mosaic of love shines oh so bright.
With each embrace, a story's told,
A tapestry rich, woven in gold.

Through trials faced, we learn to bend,
In every struggle, it's love we send.
Faithful anchors in roughest seas,
In unity strong, we find our peace.

The echoes of kindness, soft and warm,
In every heartbeat, a shelter from harm.
In the dance of life, we find our way,
Heart-made bonds, forever stay.

Together we flourish, roots intertwined,
In the garden of trust, love's gently lined.
Through all the seasons, we'll always find,
The heart-made bonds that forever bind.

Side by Side with Myself

In the quiet stillness, I learn to be,
A friend to my spirit, just me and me.
No mirrors to judge, no voices to sway,
Side by side, I embrace the day.

With every heartbeat, courage awakes,
In comforting whispers, the fear slowly breaks.
Under the stars, I find my light,
Together we wander, through dark and bright.

A dance of acceptance, shadows unite,
I cherish my flaws, embrace every fight.
In solitude's grace, I learn to feel,
Side by side, my heart starts to heal.

Through valleys of doubt, we gently tread,
With kindness and love, doubts fade instead.
In the tapestry woven, threads intertwine,
Side by side, my soul, so divine.

With every heartbeat, the journey unfolds,
In the warmth of my spirit, a story retold.
Side by side, I find peace within,
Together we flourish, the dance to begin.

The Colors of My Interior

In the palette of feelings, hues collide,
Bright yellows of joy, where dreams reside.
Deep blues of sorrow, wash over the grey,
The colors of my interior, dance and play.

With strokes of courage, I paint the dawn,
Each shade a reminder that life carries on.
Crimson of passion ignites the soul,
In shades of my essence, I become whole.

The greens of healing, gentle and bright,
Brush away shadows, inviting the light.
Each emotion a language, no words can confine,
The colors of my interior, uniquely divine.

In the canvas of moments, I sketch my truth,
Tangerine laughter, the spirit of youth.
Through artful expression, I set my heart free,
My inner landscape, a rhapsody.

With every hue whispered, I boldly proclaim,
In the story of colors, love's always the same.
The strokes of my spirit eternally beam,
The colors of my interior, a vibrant dream.

Seeds of Self-Compassion

In the soil of kindness, I plant my heart,
Tiny seeds of love, a hopeful start.
Watered with patience, they begin to bloom,
Roots of compassion dissolve all the gloom.

With gentle whispers, I nurture my soul,
Believing in progress, I learn to be whole.
Through storms and struggles, I stand tall and brave,
The seeds of my worth, I tenderly save.

In the garden of moments, I laugh and I cry,
Cultivating growth as the days flutter by.
Each tender shoot whispers, "You're enough,"
The seeds of self-compassion, strong and tough.

Embracing the shadows, I learn to forgive,
In the light of acceptance, I truly live.
From the depths of my heart, a new joy will sprout,
Seeds of self-compassion, a love I've found out.

As blossoms unfold, my spirit takes flight,
In the warmth of my garden, everything feels right.
With every new dawn, my heart starts to see,
The seeds of self-compassion, forever in me.

Heartfelt Moments of Clarity

In whispers soft, I find the light,
A spark ignites, dispelling night.
In silence pure, my thoughts emerge,
A tide of calm, a gentle surge.

With every breath, I feel the flow,
Awakening truths I long to know.
A moment brief, yet deeply felt,
Where fears dissolve, and hope is dealt.

The world stands still, my heart beats clear,
In fleeting time, I shed each fear.
A vision bright, a path unveiled,
In clarity's grace, I'm never jailed.

I grasp the threads of what is real,
Embracing the joy that I can feel.
These moments rich, they shape my soul,
In heartfelt peace, I find my role.

So here I stand, in vibrant hue,
And cherish all, both old and new.
In clarity's arms, I softly sway,
Each heartbeat sings, my truth will stay.

The Echo of My Genuine Self

In shadows cast, my spirit roams,
Through echoes deep, I find my homes.
With every verse, a tale to tell,
In honesty's grasp, I know so well.

The whispers soft, they call my name,
In every note, a spark, a flame.
Reflecting back, I see the light,
The essence true, within my sight.

As sounds collide, and silence breaks,
My genuine self, the echo wakes.
With every heartbeat, I understand,
The chords of life, a guiding hand.

In joyful tones, I find my song,
A melody where I belong.
In every note, a piece of me,
The echo pure, forever free.

So let me sing, let voices blend,
In harmony, where souls transcend.
This echo strong, my heart's refrain,
In genuine light, I rise again.

Embracing the Inner Universe

Within my heart, a cosmos spins,
With endless wonders, life begins.
In quiet realms, my spirit soars,
Exploring depths, through unseen doors.

Galaxies dance in thoughts so bright,
Stars align in the velvety night.
With every pulse, creation swells,
A universe where joy compels.

The silence speaks, the stillness sings,
In every breath, my spirit clings.
To boundless skies where dreams unfold,
In whispered truths, I find the bold.

I journey through this vast expanse,
Embracing all, a cosmic dance.
In inner realms, I seek and find,
The universe, a mirror of mind.

So here I stand, a stardust spark,
Embracing light, igniting dark.
In every heartbeat, I explore,
The inner universe, forevermore.

A Sanctuary of Self-Reflection

In tranquil space, I pause and breathe,
A sanctuary where I believe.
With gentle thoughts, I find my way,
In stalwart peace, I choose to stay.

Mirrored waters, calm and bright,
Reflecting depths, I seek the light.
With every ripple, wisdom flows,
In self-reflection, my spirit grows.

The stillness whispers, secrets shared,
In quiet corners, love is bared.
I sift through dreams, both near and far,
In this embrace, I see my star.

With patient grace, I face each fear,
Unraveling truths, I hold most dear.
In every glance, authenticity,
In sanctuary's heart, I find me.

So here I dwell, within my shell,
Embracing all, both dark and swell.
A haven sweet, where I reflect,
A sanctuary of self-respect.

Echoes of Affection

In whispers soft, your voice I hear,
The warmth of love, so crystal clear.
In every glance, a story told,
With every beat, our hearts unfold.

Through tangled paths, we laugh and play,
In shared moments, we find our way.
Like stars that dance in endless night,
Our souls entwined, forever bright.

With gentle hands, we mold our fate,
In sacred trust, we navigate.
The echoes linger, sweet and true,
In every breath, I cherish you.

In secret corners, we find our space,
In silent vows, our hearts embrace.
Through trials faced and joy we share,
Our love endures, beyond compare.

So let the world fade into gray,
Together, dear, we'll find our way.
In every heartbeat, in every sigh,
Our love's a dream that will not die.

Harmony Within

In stillness found, a soft refrain,
Within the heart, a gentle pain.
We seek the peace, the quiet grace,
In every line, our truth we trace.

Like rivers flow, we drift and bend,
In perfect tune, our souls ascend.
With every note, our spirits sing,
Together, we embrace the spring.

Through symphonies of dusk and dawn,
In whispered dreams, our hopes are drawn.
With every laugh and shared embrace,
We find our rhythm, in this space.

The world outside may twist and turn,
Yet in our hearts, the fire burns.
A melody that intertwines,
In harmony, our love aligns.

So let the music rise and swell,
In every moment, all is well.
With every heartbeat, hand in hand,
We'll dance upon this sacred land.

Garden of Intimacy

In secret gardens, love does bloom,
With fragrant petals, dispelling gloom.
In whispered winds, our secrets flow,
In tender moments, feelings grow.

We weave a world of trust and care,
Where every glance ignites the air.
Through sunlit days and starlit nights,
In shared silence, our hearts ignite.

With every touch, a spark we share,
In lush embrace, we strip us bare.
For in this space, we come alive,
Our souls entwined, forever thrive.

The blossoms dance, a soft caress,
In fragrant blooms, we find our rest.
With every heartbeat, every sigh,
In this garden, love won't die.

So let us tend this sacred ground,
In every laugh, pure joy is found.
Together we will plant and sow,
In the garden of our love, we grow.

Reflection in a Gentle Mirror

In quiet moments, I see your face,
A tender smile, a warm embrace.
In every glance, a truth revealed,
In gentle mirrors, our hearts are healed.

The world may shift, the tides may change,
Yet in this bond, we find no range.
With every echo, every tear,
In whispered love, I hold you near.

Through sunlit paths and shadows cast,
In each reflection, our love holds fast.
With every heartbeat, time stands still,
In quiet whispers, we find our will.

The gentle mirror brings us close,
In softest light, we find our dose.
With every story, woven tight,
In every dawn, we chase the light.

So let us dance in this sweet space,
In harmony, we find our grace.
In all the echoes, I hear your call,
In gentle mirrors, we have it all.

Heartfelt Essence

In whispers soft, love flows anew,
A gentle touch, like morning dew,
Through tangled paths, our spirits soar,
In every heartbeat, I feel you more.

The warmth of sun on tender skin,
Echoes of laughter deep within,
A symphony of silent cries,
Awakening truths beneath the skies.

Together we dance in twilight's glow,
As shadows fade, our feelings grow,
Time stands still in this sweet embrace,
In heartbeats shared, we find our place.

With every glance, a story told,
In every sigh, a love so bold,
Interwoven dreams, a tapestry,
In your eyes, I find the key.

Forever bound, through joy and pain,
In stormy clouds, you are my rain,
A bond unbroken, strong and true,
In every heartbeat, I choose you.

Blooming from Within

Petals unfold in morning light,
Softly whispering sweet delight,
Each moment cherished, nature's sign,
A quiet strength, a heart divine.

Amidst the thorns, we find our grace,
In every bud, a hidden space,
Blooming gently, fearless too,
The world awakens, fresh and new.

Colors bursting, vibrant, bright,
With every breeze, pure joy in sight,
In unity, we find our way,
With love to guide us, come what may.

Roots entwined beneath the ground,
In silent whispers, even found,
A garden flourishing, side by side,
In our hearts, we safely hide.

Together we face the changing skies,
With open hearts and hopeful eyes,
Blooming fiercely, let us grow,
In the light of love, our truth we show.

Hidden Currents of Care

Beneath the surface, feelings flow,
A quiet current, soft and low,
In each small act, a truth revealed,
In heart's deep waters, love concealed.

Gentle gestures, a knowing glance,
In shared silence, hearts find dance,
The little things, they speak so loud,
Binding us close, a sacred shroud.

Even in darkness, love will shine,
Through shadowed valleys, we align,
With every ripple, we collide,
In tenderness, we can't divide.

Whispers echo in the night,
Wrapped in warmth, we find the light,
In unseen ties that softly bind,
Hidden currents that don't unwind.

With every heartbeat, still we care,
In unspoken words, a love so rare,
Together we navigate the sea,
In hidden currents, you are with me.

Warmth Beneath the Skin

Fingers linger on weathered lace,
Tracing maps of time and space,
In every touch, a story spun,
In the silence, two become one.

Nestled close, with hearts aglow,
In shared moments, we let love grow,
Through gentle sighs and fleeting laughs,
We weave our dreams with tender crafts.

The world outside may shift and sway,
Yet here, our love will find its way,
Through storms and trials, side by side,
In the warmth of hearts, we confide.

Softened shadows in candlelight,
Hold me close, the world feels right,
With every heartbeat, warm and true,
In this embrace, it's just us two.

Endless nights and golden dawns,
In your arms, my spirit yawns,
A lifetime promised, skin to skin,
In every heartbeat, love begins.

Echoes of Self-Discovery

In shadows deep where secrets dwell,
A whisper calls, a silent bell.
Through tangled paths I wander wide,
Each step I take, my past beside.

With every breath, a truth unspooled,
Fragments of dreams, once tightly ruled.
I trace the lines of who I've been,
Awakening the strength within.

The mirror holds my gaze anew,
Reflections shift in vibrant hue.
A tapestry of scars and grace,
Each mark a tale I now embrace.

Through valleys low and mountains tall,
I learn to rise, to heed the call.
The echo of my heart's own song,
Guides me forth where I belong.

As dawn unfolds, a canvas bright,
I paint my dreams in morning light.
The journey's paved with honest tears,
Each step I take dispels my fears.

Radiant Reflections

In quiet pools the light will dance,
Each ripple holds a fleeting chance.
Mirrored skies and whispers soft,
Dreams of gold in hearts aloft.

The sun embraces every thought,
In brightness found, battles fought.
With open arms, I greet the day,
Radiant truths in bright array.

A moment caught, a breath divine,
In stillness, stars and thoughts align.
Textures woven through the air,
Shimmering hopes, all laid bare.

I gather light like golden thread,
Weaving warmth in what is said.
Reflections bloom in vibrant tones,
In every glance, a heart atones.

Shadows fade, the past released,
In radiant love, my soul's increased.
I dance within this lighted space,
Embracing all, my truest grace.

Nurturing the Soul's Garden

In gentle earth, where seedlings sprout,
I tend to dreams, uproot doubt.
With every hand, a loving touch,
Cultivating hopes that mean so much.

The tendrils reach for skies above,
Each blossom sings the song of love.
With patience' hand, I water deep,
In nurturing, my heart will leap.

Through storms and sun, the garden grows,
Lessons learned in ebb and flow.
Each season brings a breath anew,
In vibrant hues, my spirit grew.

I plant the seeds of kindness wide,
In every heart, let love reside.
With roots entwined, we share this space,
Together, bloom in sweet embrace.

As petals fall, new life begins,
In cycles found, the joy within.
I cherish all, the weeds and flowers,
Nurturing strengths through life's long hours.

Warm Whispers of Authenticity

In hushed tones the truth takes flight,
A gentle breeze, soft as the night.
With open arms, I hear the call,
To be myself, to risk it all.

Each whispered word a sacred vow,
To honor self in every now.
In genuine hues, my heart will sing,
Authentic joys that freedom bring.

Through careful steps, I find my way,
In honest paths, no need to sway.
The warmth of being, pure and bright,
Illuminates my inner light.

With every heartbeat, I embrace,
The flaws and strengths that fill this space.
Authenticity, my guiding star,
No masks required, just who we are.

In every glance, a story told,
Warm whispers shared, like threads of gold.
With courage found, I stand so clear,
In the wild wind, I venture near.

Deep Within

In shadows deep, the whispers stir,
A hidden path where dreams occur.
Through silent halls, my heart will roam,
In the stillness, I find home.

Beneath the weight of thoughts untold,
The strength within begins to unfold.
With every breath, a story grows,
In the quiet, my spirit knows.

The echoes call, they pull me near,
To face the truths I often fear.
As layers peel, I start to see,
The light that lives inside of me.

A journey deep, yet oh so clear,
Through sacred depths, I persevere.
With every step, I feel the grace,
Of knowing my true, sacred space.

Love Awakens

In gentle hearts, a spark ignites,
Awakening souls on starry nights.
With tender words, the silence stirs,
In every glance, the longing purrs.

Two hands entwined, a promise made,
In the warmth of love, fears fade.
With every heartbeat, passion swells,
In whispers soft, the spirit dwells.

Through laughter shared and tears that fall,
Love covers us, a woven shawl.
In moments small, the magic glows,
As time stands still, our story flows.

With open hearts, we dare to soar,
In love's embrace, we're evermore.
United souls, a dance so true,
In every hue, I see you.

The Quiet Strength of Self

In solitude, I find my place,
With gentle thoughts, I embrace grace.
The world may swirl, yet here I stand,
A silent force, a steady hand.

Through trials faced, I learn to rise,
With courage found in silent eyes.
In every challenge, wisdom grows,
In stillness deep, my spirit flows.

The whispers of the heart remain,
Through storms of doubt, I shed the pain.
Embracing flaws, I come alive,
In self-acceptance, I will thrive.

With roots that ground, I stand so tall,
In every heartbeat, I hear the call.
The quiet strength, my guiding light,
With every breath, I claim my might.

Vibrations of True Connection

In laughter shared, our souls align,
In every gaze, a spark divine.
The energy that flows between,
Creates a bond, pure and serene.

With open hearts, we speak our truth,
In moments real, we find our youth.
Each touch ignites a vibrant flame,
In every heartbeat, love's refrain.

The harmony we create anew,
Resonates in shades of blue.
In whispered dreams, we intertwine,
Our spirits dance, a sacred sign.

Through time and space, we journey on,
In every dawn, our spirits spawn.
The vibrations strong, we will not sway,
In connection true, we find our way.

Secrets of the Soul's Garden

In shadows deep, the blossoms bloom,
Their fragrant whispers chase the gloom.
The whispers hold, untold delight,
In every petal, dark and light.

Among the trees, the secrets hide,
In every breath, the truths abide.
Through twisted paths, I wander slow,
To find the seeds of what I know.

With gentle hands, I nurture dreams,
And let the sunlight grace the streams.
In fertile grounds, my spirit grows,
Among the thorns, the beauty shows.

The garden speaks, a language pure,
In every heart, a silken lure.
With every tear and joy combined,
The secrets of my soul unwind.

Heartbeats of Self-Nurture

In quiet moments, I take a breath,
Embracing the stillness that whispers my worth.
Gentle whispers cradle my soul,
Awakening dreams, making me whole.

I plant seeds of kindness in my heart,
Watering hope, a nurturing art.
With every heartbeat, I learn to see,
The beauty in simply being me.

Through shadows of doubt, I softly tread,
Filling my spirit with words unsaid.
I gather my thoughts, like petals they bloom,
Creating a garden that banishes gloom.

I treasure each moment, a sacred gift,
Learning to love and to gently uplift.
In the mirror's glance, I find my grace,
A reflection of strength in a tender space.

As time flows by, I stand in my light,
Embracing my journey, my heart taking flight.
In the chambers of nurture, I find my way,
In the heartbeats of love, I choose to stay.

The Symphony of Self-Belief

A chorus of courage begins to rise,
Harmonizing dreams beneath endless skies.
With every note, my spirit grows strong,
In the melody of self, I find where I belong.

Each challenge I face, a step on my path,
Crafting my song, embracing the wrath.
In the silence, I hear my heart's tune,
A symphony building, rising like a moon.

The rhythm of hope conducts my way,
Guiding my footsteps, come what may.
In unity with self, the music plays loud,
Turning my fears into a thrumming crowd.

With strings of passion, I weave my fate,
Composing a life that I celebrate.
In echoes of doubt, I find my refrain,
The symphony of me will always remain.

As the conductor, I wield my might,
Orchestrating dreams that glitter in sight.
Every crescendo, a call to believe,
In the symphony of self, I dare to achieve.

Hidden Treasures of the Heart

In the depths of silence, treasures reside,
Gems of wisdom, my heart's quiet guide.
With each gentle moment, I seek and I find,
The hidden wonders that life has aligned.

Fragments of joy like sunlight will gleam,
Shimmering softly, a comforting dream.
In the chaos of life, I pause and reflect,
Finding the riches that love can collect.

Embracing the shadows, I unveil my grace,
In the corners of solitude, I find my place.
With kindness as compass, I wander and roam,
Discovering treasures deep within my home.

The map of my heart is drawn with affection,
Leading me onward, in sweet introspection.
I gather the fragments, stories untold,
Revealing the treasures more precious than gold.

In each gentle heartbeat, I cherish and hold,
The hidden treasures in experiences bold.
A tapestry woven with love, I impart,
The greatest fortune lies deep in the heart.

A Journey to Inner Harmony

With every sunrise, I start anew,
Seeking balance in all that I do.
A dance of spirit, my journey unfolds,
In the whispers of peace, my heart gently molds.

I wander through meadows, where stillness breeds,
Harvesting moments that nourish my needs.
In the gentle embrace of a calm, clear stream,
I find my direction, I follow my dream.

The path may be winding, with lessons to share,
But with each step, I grow wise and aware.
In the mirror of nature, I see my true self,
As I move through the forest, a dance of good health.

In the cadence of breath, I learn to be free,
Unlocking my spirit, embracing the sea.
With every heartbeat, I align with my soul,
In the journey of healing, I finally feel whole.

As stars guide my night, I welcome the light,
In unity with all, my heart takes flight.
A journey to harmony, I embrace with delight,
For within my own essence, I discover true might.

The Quiet Roar of Confidence

In whispers bold, I stand so tall,
In shadows deep, I heed the call.
A steady heart, a silent flame,
With quiet strength, I stake my claim.

The world may doubt, but I stay true,
With every step, I push on through.
With dreams that soar and fears that fade,
In this vast light, my soul won't fade.

Each little win, a roaring sound,
In silence, strength and hopes abound.
With every breath, I rise anew,
The quiet roar, I break on through.

Though storms may rage and winds may blow,
In stillness, I find courage to grow.
A steady pulse, a guiding star,
In my own space, I am who I are.

The night may fall, but I will shine,
With quiet grace, I claim what's mine.
In the echoes of my heart's refrain,
The quiet roar, my sweet domain.

The Power of Being Me

In every flaw, a beauty glows,
In every scar, a strength that shows.
Unique, I stand, no need to fit,
Embracing all, I truly commit.

With laughter bright and tears that flow,
I find the light in shadows' show.
A tapestry of joy and pain,
In every thread, the truth remains.

I dance to beats that fill my soul,
In this wild world, I am whole.
With open heart, I sing aloud,
In my own skin, I stand so proud.

The whispers tell me I can't soar,
But I will rise and claim what's more.
In every breath, I feel the air,
The power swells, it's mine to share.

So here I stand, fierce and free,
A celebration of being me.
In vibrant hues, I paint my day,
With every step, I find my way.

Notes from the Heart's Refuge

In quiet moments, whispers flow,
In sacred space, the heart will know.
A gentle pulse, a soft embrace,
In every sigh, I find my place.

Each note I write, a story told,
Of love and loss, of brave and bold.
These tender strokes of ink and grace,
In every line, a warm embrace.

In shadows cast, I light a spark,
With words that heal, dispelling dark.
The heart's refuge, I claim my own,
In every tear, a seed is sown.

In whispers soft, the truth unfolds,
In every heartbeat, the story holds.
These notes I gather, pure and true,
In the heart's refuge, I find you.

So let the pages turn with time,
Each rhythm beats, a loving rhyme.
In quiet strength, I softly weave,
The notes of life, I choose to believe.

Radiance Beneath the Surface

In quiet depths, the light does gleam,
A hidden spark, a vibrant dream.
Beneath the waves, the colors dance,
In silent waters, I find my chance.

The surface calm may hide the fire,
In tranquil depths, my soul aspires.
With every breath, I dive anew,
The radiance, I claim what's true.

Where shadows play and moments hide,
A world of wonder waits inside.
With open heart, I face the flow,
The light within begins to glow.

In every ripple, wisdom flows,
In gentle waves, my courage grows.
With open arms, I embrace the light,
The radiance dawns, I take my flight.

So dive with me, into the blue,
With every heartbeat, we'll find the hue.
In depths concealed, the beauty swells,
The radiance shines, the soul compels.

Rising from the Heart's Depths

In shadows deep, we find our light,
A spark that burns through endless night.
With every breath, we chase the dawn,
From pain and doubt, a new hope's born.

Like rivers flow, our spirits rise,
In whispered dreams, the soul complies.
We lift our voices, strong and free,
Emerging from what used to be.

Through trials faced, we wear the scars,
Each mark a tale, each bruise a star.
With courage sewn into our thread,
We weave the life we seek to tread.

And though the path may twist and turn,
The fire within will always burn.
With hearts unbound, we forge our fate,
Rising high, we celebrate.

So let us stand, hand in hand,
In unity, on sacred land.
Together, strong, we'll shape our flight,
From heart's depths, we claim our light.

Illuminating the Inner Sanctuary

In quiet spaces, shadows glow,
Where thoughts take root and feelings flow.
Each flicker shines, a gentle plea,
A light within, we long to see.

Beneath the surface, treasures hide,
In stillness, we can turn the tide.
With knowing eyes, we seek the truth,
In every breath, the pulse of youth.

The walls may echo with a sigh,
Yet in this chamber, dreams can fly.
With open hearts, we gather round,
In love's embrace, our souls are found.

We shine like stars, in darkness bright,
Illuminating the endless night.
With every pulse, we celebrate,
This inner peace, our cherished fate.

So in the silence, let us dwell,
In sacred spaces, all is well.
Together, let our spirits soar,
In unity, forevermore.

Cherished Whispers of Being

In gentle hush, our hearts do speak,
In every moment, strong yet meek.
The whispers soft, like breezes play,
They guide us through each winding day.

With every glance, a story told,
In treasured bonds, we turn to gold.
These sacred ties, we hold them dear,
In love's embrace, we conquer fear.

Through laughter shared and tears we shed,
In every word, our truth is bred.
A tapestry of lives entwined,
In this dance, our souls aligned.

The moments fleeting, yet they stay,
In cherished whispers, we find our way.
With open hearts, we share our dreams,
In every tear, a silver gleam.

So let us speak in soft refrains,
Of joy and hope, through all the pains.
In unity, our voices blend,
In cherished whispers, love transcends.

Unfolding the Heart's Petals

Like blossoms bloom, we open wide,
In sunlight's warmth, we will not hide.
Each petal soft, with colors bright,
A canvas of our shared delight.

With every heartbeat, life unfolds,
In stories whispered, love retold.
The gentle breeze, our sweetest song,
In harmony, we all belong.

From seeds of hope, we rise anew,
In fragrant air, our dreams come true.
With every breath, the world we greet,
In unity, our hearts can meet.

As seasons change, we still embrace,
The fleeting moments in this space.
In every fold, a memory spans,
In love's great garden, we take stance.

So let us cherish each soft hue,
In vibrant paths, we'll journey through.
Together, we'll embrace the dawn,
Unfolding hearts in love's sweet song.

Inward Bound: A Love Story

In the quiet night we share,
Laughter falls like whispered care.
Eyes that glimmer, souls entwined,
In every heartbeat, love defined.

Through shadows deep, our dreams will roam,
Two hearts journey, finding home.
Whispers soft as morning dew,
Our stories weave, forever true.

In every glance, a spark ignites,
Stars align in joyous flights.
With gentle hands, the world we shape,
In love's embrace, there's no escape.

The road ahead may twist and bend,
Still hand in hand, we will contend.
In every storm, through trial and strife,
Together we'll unfold this life.

A love so deep, it knows no bounds,
In silence, sweetness still surrounds.
With every step, our spirits grow,
Inward bound, we learn to flow.

The Unseen Threads of Affection

Beneath the surface, love does weave,
Invisible strands we can perceive.
With gentle touch, and knowing smiles,
Our hearts connect across the miles.

In laughter shared, in silent tears,
Unseen threads bind through our fears.
With every heartbeat, a silent pact,
In the quiet moments, we interact.

A glance exchanged, a spark unseen,
Every whispered word between.
A tapestry of life we thread,
In the canvas of love, we're wed.

In storms that shake and wind that howls,
Love's strength resonates and bows.
Through trials faced and joys preserved,
Unseen threads, forever served.

When darkness lingers, shadows loom,
Love's light shines bright, dispels the gloom.
In the gentle ties that can't be broke,
Unseen threads of love still invoke.

A Mirror of the Soul

In your eyes, my heart finds peace,
Reflection deep, a sweet release.
Every glance reveals the best,
In love's embrace, we find our rest.

Through laughter's dance and sorrow's flight,
In mirrors bright, we fill the night.
Our souls connect in subtle ways,
A gentle warmth that ever stays.

Each memory forged, a shining ray,
Guiding us in soft array.
In moments shared, we dare to dream,
Two souls as one, a lasting theme.

In the quiet, truths unfold,
With every story, more to be told.
Reflecting love, our spirits whole,
You are my mirror, heart and soul.

In twilight's hush, where shadows blend,
My deepest love, my truest friend.
Together we rise, together we fall,
In this vast world, you're my all.

Threads of Heartfelt Reverie

In dreams we dance, a soft ballet,
Threads of love gently sway.
Through every heartbeat, every sigh,
In the tapestry of us, we fly.

The colors bright, the shades of night,
In every thread, a spark of light.
With every word, we realign,
In heartfelt reverie, love will shine.

In memory's quilt, we stitch the past,
Moments cherished, forever cast.
Through time and space, our hearts will sing,
In harmonious notes, our souls take wing.

Within the silence, our hearts will know,
Threads of passion begin to grow.
In every touch, in every glance,
We write our story, a timeless dance.

With every heartbeat, a rhythm sweet,
A journey shared, a love complete.
In this reverie, we find our place,
Threads of love in sweet embrace.

A Dance of Inner Light

Shadows fade, whispers play,
In the glow of dawn's first ray.
Hearts entwined, a silent song,
In this moment, we belong.

Footsteps light on fragile ground,
In the silence, love is found.
Every glance, a spark ignites,
A dance of joy, our inner lights.

With every turn, we glide and sway,
Lost in magic, come what may.
In the rhythm, we become one,
Our souls radiant, like the sun.

The world may blur outside our space,
But in this dance, we find our grace.
An eternal bond, we see it clear,
Through every sway, I hold you near.

Together now, let laughter ring,
In this dance, our spirits sing.
As the stars begin to rise,
We'll find our truth beneath the skies.

The Tender Fortress

In the quiet of a thunderstorm,
I find solace, safe and warm.
Walls built high, love's embrace,
A tender fortress, our sacred space.

Whispers shared under a roof,
In this shelter, we find proof.
Hands held tight, fears subside,
In our hearts, there's nowhere to hide.

Outside rage, but in here, peace,
Moments shared bring sweet release.
Together strong, we brave the night,
In this haven, everything's right.

The world may cast its shadows wide,
Yet here within, we stand with pride.
Every heartbeat, like a drum,
In our fortress, love will come.

Time may flow, but we stand still,
In this fortress, hearts fulfill.
Tender memories, like vines entwined,
Our fortress built, forever defined.

Chorus of the Heart

In the stillness, a soft refrain,
Echoes of love, like gentle rain.
A chorus hums beneath the skin,
The heartbeat's song, where dreams begin.

Cascading notes in twilight's glow,
A melody only we could know.
With every breath, harmonies rise,
A symphony under the skies.

Each whispered word, a vital chord,
Binding spirits, a silent accord.
United we stand, our voices blend,
In this song, our hearts transcend.

Moments linger, time stands still,
In this chorus, we find our will.
No greater magic, no finer art,
Than the music from the heart.

Dance with me in this sacred sound,
Together, forever, bliss profound.
In every beat, our story's told,
A chorus of love, to have and hold.

Beneath the Layers

Beneath the surface, life unfolds,
In whispers soft, a story told.
Layers peel like petals bare,
Revealing truths we find so rare.

What lies hidden, we shall seek,
In gentle touch, we hear the speak.
Fears and dreams intertwined,
Unraveling, our hearts aligned.

Voices murmur in the dark,
As we unravel every spark.
In this dance of depths explored,
Every layer, a treasure stored.

Time will show, like seasons change,
Layers shift, yet hearts remain.
With every truth, our bond will grow,
Revealing love, like rivers flow.

So take my hand, let's journey deep,
In each layer, secrets keep.
Together we dive, without the fears,
In this hidden world, our love appears.

Love Flourishes

In the garden where we stand,
Love flourishes, hand in hand.
Petals open, colors bright,
In this bloom, we find our light.

Seeds once sown in tender care,
Grow into dreams we gladly share.
With every sunbeam, hearts will soar,
In this love, we crave for more.

Through every storm and gentle breeze,
Together rooted, we find ease.
Nurtured by laughter, softened by tears,
In this garden, we conquer fears.

Time may weather, yet we embrace,
Seasons change but leave their trace.
In each blossom's fleeting sigh,
Our love's a dance that will not die.

So let us plant, our hopes in rows,
And watch in awe how sweetness grows.
In this haven, our hearts align,
Love flourishes, forever divine.

Waves of Inner Resilience

In the storm of life, I stand my ground,
Rising like the tide, I won't back down.
Though the winds may howl, my spirit stays,
I embrace the waves, in so many ways.

Each crash of salt, a whisper inside,
Reminding me gently, I'll not subside.
Through trials and tests, I learn to soar,
The ocean of strength forevermore.

With every ripple, I gather my might,
In the darkest depths, I find my light.
Beneath the surface, my courage swims,
I'll ride the currents, despite the whims.

So let the seas churn, let the waters rage,
I'll write my story on nature's page.
For each wave that crashes, I'll stand anew,
In the dance of resilience, I find my cue.

And when the calm comes after the storm,
I'll cherish the peace that starts to form.
With every tide, I grow and expand,
Waves of resilience, I proudly withstand.

Heartfelt Echoes of Peace

In quiet moments, my heart will speak,
With whispers of love, both soft and meek.
The echoes of peace in the still of night,
Guide my weary soul, bring gentle light.

The world outside may often rage,
Yet within, I turn a sacred page.
Each breath I take, a soothing balm,
Cradling my spirit, wrapping in calm.

Through valleys deep and mountains high,
I seek the grace in every sigh.
In gardens where serenity grows,
I plant the seeds that the heart knows.

With every sunrise, a chance to renew,
To let compassion's colors break through.
In the tapestry of life, I weave,
Heartfelt echoes of peace, I believe.

And when the world's noise seems too loud,
I'll find my refuge, a silent shroud.
For in every beat, my soul finds release,
An embrace of love, my truest peace.

The Essence of Who I Am

Beneath the surface, where shadows play,
Lies the essence of me, in every ray.
With roots entwined in the rich, dark soil,
I blossom and grow, despite life's toil.

In mirrors reflecting, I see my truth,
The dreams of my youth, my eternal sleuth.
Every scar tells a story, a chapter passed,
In the book of my life, each moment will last.

I dance with the stars, I breathe with the trees,
In harmony woven, carried by the breeze.
With open arms, I embrace my flaws,
For they are the threads that support my cause.

In the tapestry of existence, I play my part,
A symphony crafted from love and art.
The essence of who I am shines bright,
A beacon of hope in the deepest night.

I surrender to growth, both big and small,
For every experience helps me stand tall.
In the realm of being, I quietly stand,
The essence of me, forever unplanned.

Shining Through Shadows

In the depths of darkness, I find my way,
A flicker of hope, a brightening ray.
Though shadows may linger, I rise with grace,
Casting my light in this sacred space.

With every challenge, I learn to see,
The beauty in struggle, it sets me free.
The night may be long, the path unclear,
Yet I hold the courage to persevere.

Embracing my fears, I stand and fight,
Transforming my doubts into pure delight.
In the canvas of life, I paint my dreams,
Shining through shadows with radiant beams.

For every whisper of sorrow and pain,
I'll rise like the sun and dance in the rain.
In the heart of the storm, I craft my song,
A melody woven, where I belong.

With each step forward, I blaze my trail,
A spirit unbroken that will not fail.
In the symphony of life, I reclaim my voice,
Shining through shadows, I rejoice.

Symphony of the Spirit

In quiet moments, whispers play,
Notes of grace in soft ballet.
Harmonies weave through air so light,
A dance of souls, both day and night.

Echoes of laughter, echoes of tears,
Carry the hopes, dissolve the fears.
Each heartbeat pulses, a rhythmic song,
Binding us close, where we all belong.

Fields of silence, where dreams take flight,
Stars awaken, shatter the night.
Melodies rise, a gentle tide,
Guiding us home to the love inside.

In every struggle, a lesson learned,
The fire ignites, the spirit burned.
Together we stand, hands intertwined,
In this symphony, our hearts aligned.

So let the music forever flow,
In waves of peace, let kindness grow.
For in our hearts, a song we share,
A timeless echo, forever fair.

Veins of Compassion

Beneath the surface, a river flows,
A gentle pulse, where kindness grows.
In hidden corners, it seeks to find,
A bridge to connect the hearts and minds.

Through trials faced, an open hand,
In every tear, a new hope planned.
Threads of mercy, woven so tight,
Illuminate shadows, turn wrong to right.

In every story, a heartbeat lies,
A spark of warmth in weary eyes.
Compassion's touch heals pain concealed,
A tender heart, forever revealed.

From kindness sown, a garden thrives,
In every act, the spirit strives.
Let love be the air that all can breathe,
As we embrace, our hearts believe.

Together we stand, a united stance,
In veins of compassion, we take a chance.
For every moment shared, we create,
A world of hope, where love annihilates.

Light Emanating from Depths

In the shadows, where silence creeps,
A flicker sparks, as the darkness weeps.
From deep within, the flames arise,
A beacon bright, beneath the skies.

Through inner journeys and trials faced,
A warmth ignites, no fears embraced.
Each step forward, a glimmer that's bold,
Fearless hearts, with stories told.

When hope feels lost, and dreams seem dim,
That inner glow begins to brim.
Against the tide, from depths we call,
The light within, it conquers all.

In moments still, when chaos reigns,
The heart erupts, releasing chains.
Let every shadow, no matter how deep,
Be kissed by light, as the soul takes a leap.

For in the depths, the spirit gleams,
A surge of love, a dance of dreams.
Seek the light, and it shall blend,
With every heartbeat, beauty transcends.

The Hidden Garden of Emotions

In whispered breezes, secrets bloom,
A landscape rich, dispelling gloom.
Roots intertwined in soft embrace,
The hidden garden, our sacred space.

With petals vibrant, colors bright,
Each feeling holds a story's light.
Joy dances freely, sorrow hides,
In this haven, the heart resides.

From laughter's roots to shadows' shade,
Every emotion, beautifully laid.
Seeds of hope in the ground we place,
Cultivating love, an endless grace.

As seasons shift, and storms may come,
We nurture truth, till peace is won.
In silence moments, growth reveals,
The depth of love that gently heals.

So wander freely through this land,
Embrace each feeling, hand in hand.
In the hidden garden, let us find,
The beauty woven in humankind.

Printed in the USA
CPSIA information can be obtained
at www.ICGtesting.com
LVHW021541261024
794861LV00009B/112